SandCastle™

Perfect Pets

Frisky Ferrets

Kelly Doudna
AUTHOR

C.A. Nobens
ILLUSTRATOR

Consulting Editor, Diane Craig, M.A./Reading Specialist

ABDO
Publishing Company

Published by ABDO Publishing Company, 4940 Viking Drive, Edina, Minnesota 55435.

Printed in the United States.

CREDITS

Edited by: Pam Price

Concept Development: Nancy Tuminelly

Cover and Interior Design and Production: Mighty Media

Photo Credits: Eyewire Images, Decante Frédéric/BIOS/Peter Arnold, Inc., Klein & Hubert/BIOS/Peter Arnold, Inc., Photodisc, ShutterStock

LIBRARY OF CONGRESS CATALOGING-IN-PUBLICATION DATA

Doudna, Kelly, 1963-
  Frisky ferrets / Kelly Doudna ; illustrated by C.A. Nobens.
     p. cm. -- (Perfect pets)
  ISBN-13: 978-1-59928-748-5 (alk. paper)
  ISBN-10: 1-59928-748-X (alk. paper)
  1. Ferrets as pets--Juvenile literature. I. Nobens, C. A. II. Title.

  SF459.F47D68 2007
  636.976'628--dc22
                                    2006033257

SandCastle™ books are created by a professional team of educators, reading specialists, and content developers around five essential components—phonemic awareness, phonics, vocabulary, text comprehension, and fluency—to assist young readers as they develop reading skills and strategies and increase their general knowledge. All books are written, reviewed, and leveled for guided reading, early reading intervention, and Accelerated Reader® programs for use in shared, guided, and independent reading and writing activities to support a balanced approach to literacy instruction.

SandCastle Level: Transitional

LET US KNOW

SandCastle would like to hear your stories about reading this book. What is your favorite page? Was there something hard that you needed help with? Share the ups and downs of learning to read. We want to hear from you! To get posted on the ABDO Publishing Company Web site, send us e-mail at:

sandcastle@abdopublishing.com

FERRETS

Ferrets are friendly, playful, and curious. Many people think they are fun pets because they are so frisky.

Kaylee makes sure her ferret's cage has a cozy sling to nap in. Ferrets sleep about 18 hours a day.

Lucas takes his ferret for a walk on a leash. Ferrets should exercise outside their cages for a little while each day.

Amanda gives her ferret food and water. Ferrets like to eat several small meals each day.

Isaiah takes his ferret to the veterinarian for a checkup. The vet listens to the ferret's heart.

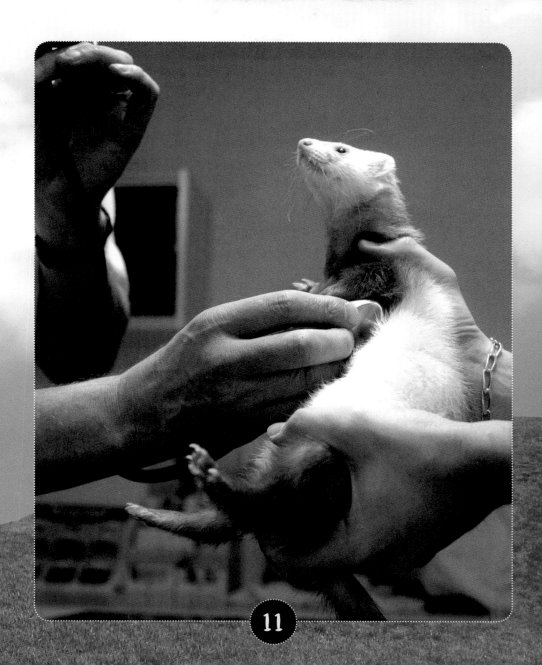

Jenna cuddles and plays with her ferret. Ferrets like lots of attention from their owners.

A Ferret Story

Garrett and his ferret
play all day.
The ferret is frisky.
Her name is Faye.

Their favorite game
is hide-and-seek.
Faye hides and
Garrett counts.
He doesn't peek.

Garrett finds Faye
under the couch.
She's so far back
that he has to crouch.

20

Faye crawls out and climbs into Garrett's lap. She's tired from playing. It's time for a nap!

Fun facts

Ferrets are in the same animal family as badgers, wolverines, skunks, sea otters, and weasels.

Female ferrets are called jills, and male ferrets are called hobs. Baby ferrets are called kits.

A group of ferrets is called a business.

In the late 1800s, Queen Victoria of England raised ferrets and gave them to people as gifts.

Glossary

attention – the act of concentrating on or giving careful thought to something.

checkup – a routine examination by a doctor.

crouch – to stoop or bend low to the ground.

cuddle – to hug or hold close.

curious – eager to learn more.

meal – the portion of food eaten at breakfast, lunch, or dinner.

veterinarian – a doctor who takes care of animals.

About SandCastle™

A professional team of educators, reading specialists, and content developers created the SandCastle™ series to support young readers as they develop reading skills and strategies and increase their general knowledge. The SandCastle™ series has four levels that correspond to early literacy development in young children. The levels are provided to help teachers and parents select appropriate books for young readers.

Emerging Readers
(no flags)

Beginning Readers
(1 flag)

Transitional Readers
(2 flags)

Fluent Readers
(3 flags)

These levels are meant only as a guide. All levels are subject to change.

ABDO
Publishing Company

To see a complete list of SandCastle™ books and other nonfiction titles from ABDO Publishing Company, visit **www.abdopublishing.com** or contact us at: 4940 Viking Drive, Edina, Minnesota 55435 • 1-800-800-1312 • fax: 1-952-831-1632